Sally Swain was born in 1958 in Sydney. After tak[...] at Sydney University, she travelled Europe and h[...] as a freelance illustrator.

Sally Swain

GREAT
HOUSEWIVES
OF ART

GRAFTON BOOKS

A Division of the Collins Publishing Group

LONDON GLASGOW
TORONTO SYDNEY AUCKLAND

Grafton Books
A Division of the Collins Publishing Group
8 Grafton Street, London W1X 3LA

A Grafton Paperback Original 1988

ISBN 0-586-20530-6

Printed and bound in Great Britain

Set in Garamond

GREAT
HOUSEWIVES
OF ART

Mad about Munch

I ARRIVED in a jolly mood at the Munch exhibition at the National Gallery and was quickly reduced to glumly walking beside pictures which revealed the gloomy Norwegian's mental state. Only perhaps Van Gogh was so evidently crazy, but at least his pictures were a celebration of life.

I asked Neil MacGregor, the gallery's director, whether the exhibition was proving popular. Munch, he said, is a great favourite with adolescents, who appear to recognise in his work some of their own mental turmoil. Adults, it seems, can find all the gloom they need in newspapers or on television.

for
Iris, David, Jennie
and Riju

Introduction

A LETTER TO THE WORLD OF ART

This morning, in between baking the pot plants and ironing the kids, strange thoughts popped into my head.

My husband, Art Extraordinaire, is a great painter, right? I spend all my time tied to the house, toiling away for him and the kids. Well, without me, he wouldn't be free to *be* Mr Art Extraordinaire. So, why doesn't he give me a little recognition and paint what I do around the house as wife, mother and home-maker? . . .

Soon after, while reheating yesterday's cupboard, I thought: how silly of me! My day is full of boring, trivial, repetitive, mindless and often pointless tasks. Who wants to look at pictures of those? After vacuuming the vegetables, I settled down to a good, long five-minute tea-break. Further questions troubled my previously disinfected and waterlogged brain.

Why don't women win medals for the cleanest, best-kept bathroom, or book-prizes for outstanding shopping lists? Is it true that women do *more* housework now than before the invention of labour-saving devices? and that men still do a negligible amount? Why don't art galleries display more images of modern woman's daily domestic grind? Isn't this worthy of painting? Anyway, so much recent art is obscure and inaccessible – must this be so?

Is it possible to bridge the gap between high and popular art? Why is great art so often the size of a wall and not a postcard? Can art be visually appealing, humorous *and* have a social message? Why, with so many female art students, do we *still* know of very few great women artists? And take the women behind the great male artists – what do we know of their lives?

Goodness me! I quite lost myself in this flood of thoughts and entirely forgot Art's shoes bubbling away on the stove.

Don't get me wrong. I believe that Art and his friends and predecessors have created truly great work and enriched our ways of seeing. But it's also important to present other possibilities.

Forty of these other possibilities have been produced by Sally Swain. But now, back to the housework.

A Housewife of Art.

Mrs Wood Hopes the Toast Won't Burn

Mrs Manet Entertains in the Garden

Mrs Bacon Bakes a Cake

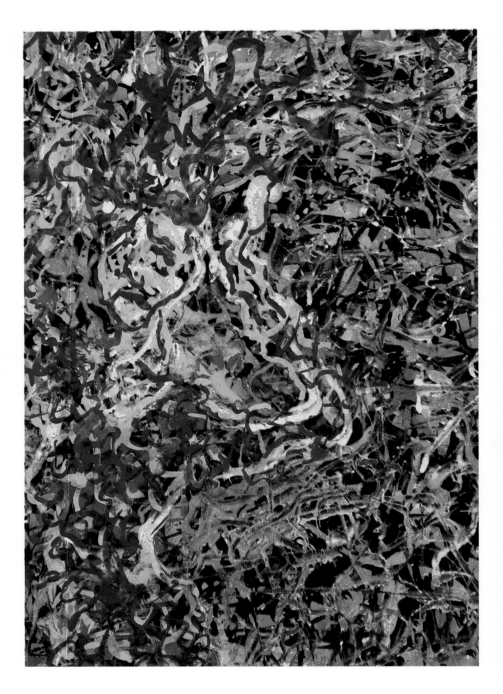

Mrs Pollock Can't Seem to Find Anything Any More

Mrs Degas Vacuums the Floor

Mrs Magritte Tidies the Hat Rack

Mrs Beardsley Won't Go to *That* Butcher Again!

Mrs Dali Hangs Out the Washing

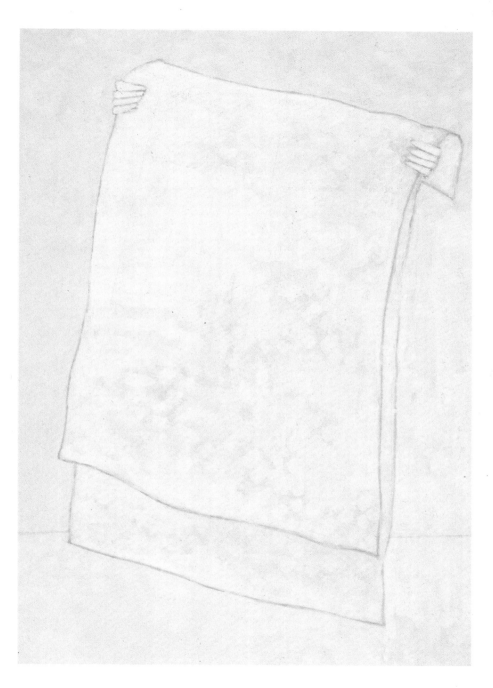

Mrs Malevich Bleaches the Sheets

Mrs Kandinsky Puts Away the Kids' Toys

Mrs Lichtenstein Sobs . . .

Mrs Monet Cleans the Pool

Mrs Chagall Feeds the Baby

Mrs Kirchner Files Her Face Every Morning

Mrs Dufy Runs a Bath

Mrs Klimt Sews a Patchwork Quilt

Mrs Toulouse-Lautrec Cleans the Toilet

Mrs Seurat Adjusts the TV Set

Mrs Renoir Cleans the Oven

Mrs Gauguin Has a Tupperware Party

Mrs Rouault Washes the Kitchen Window

Mrs Braque Sets the Table for Dinner, While Playing the Violin

Mrs Nolan Posts a Letter

Mrs Daumier Takes Out the Garbage

Mrs de Chirico Feels Agoraphobic

Mrs Klee Cleans Out the Bird Cage

Mrs Modigliani Relaxes After a Long Day

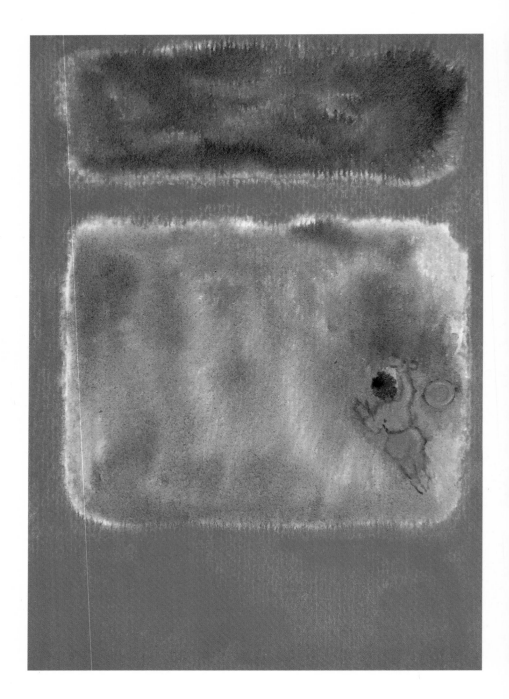

Mrs Rothko Scrubs the Carpet

Mrs Arp Reads the Paper (According to the Laws of Chance)

Mrs Mondrian Mops the Floor

Mrs Matisse Polishes the Goldfish

Mrs Miro Sweeps the Floor

Mrs van Gogh Makes the Bed

Mrs Leger Makes Carrot Juice

Mrs Duchamp Rids Herself of Those Unsightly Facial Hairs

Mrs Warhol Doesn't Like Cooking Dinner